MOTHMAN

This series features unsolved mysteries, urban legends, and other curious stories. Each creepy, shocking, or befuddling book focuses on what people believe and hear. True or not? That's for you to decide!

45th Parallel Press

Published in the United States of America by Cherry Lake Publishing
Ann Arbor, Michigan
www.cherrylakepublishing.com

Author: Virginia Loh-Hagan
Reading Adviser: Marla Conn MS, Ed., Literacy specialist, Read-Ability, Inc.
Book Designer: Felicia Macheske

Photo Credits: © Zsolt Biczo/Shutterstock.com, cover; © Ninell/Shutterstock.com, cover; © Susilyn/Shutterstock.com, 5; © Rawpixel.com/Shutterstock.com, 7; © baranq/Shutterstock.com, 8; © Blend Images/Shutterstock.com, 11; © Photographee.eu/Shutterstock.com, 12; © Dmitrijs Bindemanis/Shutterstock.com, 15; © David Malik/Shutterstock.com, 17; © Luis Louro/Shutterstock.com, 18; © Vitaliy Holovin/Shutterstock.com, 20; © Richie Diesterheft/Flickr.com/CC BY 2.0, 23; © Joseph Sohm/Shutterstock.com, 24; © Centrill Media/Shutterstock.com, 27; © Zurijeta/Shutterstock.com, 29

Graphic Elements Throughout: © iofoto/Shutterstock.com; © COLCU/Shutterstock.com; © spacedrone808/Shutterstock.com; © rf.vector.stock/Shutterstock.com; © donatas1205/Shutterstock.com; © cluckva/Shutterstock.com; © Eky Studio/Shutterstock.com

45th Parallel Press is an imprint of Cherry Lake Publishing.

Library of Congress Cataloging-in-Publication Data

Names: Loh-Hagan, Virginia, author.
Title: Mothman / by Dr. Virginia Loh-Hagan.
Description: Ann Arbor : Cherry Lake Publishing, 2018. | Series: Urban legends: Don't read alone! | Includes bibliographical references and index. | Audience: Grades 4 to 6.
Identifiers: LCCN 2017035392| ISBN 9781534107618 (hardcover) | ISBN 9781534109599 (pdf) | ISBN 9781534108608 (pbk.) | ISBN 9781534120587 (hosted ebook)
Subjects: LCSH: Mothman—Juvenile literature.
Classification: LCC QL89.2.M68 L64 2018 | DDC 001.944—dc23
LC record available at https://lccn.loc.gov/2017035392

Cherry Lake Publishing would like to acknowledge the work of The Partnership for 21st Century Skills.
Please visit *www.p21.org* for more information.

Printed in the United States of America
Corporate Graphics

TABLE OF CONTENTS

Chapter One

IT'S A BIRD!
IT'S A PLANE!
IT'S A...?

Who saw Mothman? What did they see?

On November 12, 1966, 5 men were digging a **grave**. Graves are places where dead bodies are buried. The men were in West Virginia. They said they saw a creature flying in the air. The creature looked human. It was brown. It was flying around the treetops. This is believed to be the first sighting of Mothman.

Another sighting happened three days later. There were 2 young couples. One couple was Roger and Linda Scarberry. The other couple was Steve and Mary Mallette. They were from Point Pleasant, West Virginia.

This first sighting took place about 85 miles (137 kilometers) away from Point Pleasant in Clendenin, West Virginia.

CONSIDER THE
EVIDENCE

There hasn't been any real proof of Mothman. But there have been some photos mistaken for him. An example is a photo taken in 2016. This is 50 years after the first sightings. WCHS-TV is a local news station. It published a picture of Mothman. It was taken by a man. The man didn't want to give his name. He just moved to Point Pleasant. He didn't know about the Mothman story. He was out hunting. He saw something jumping from tree to tree. He took a picture. The picture is blurry. It shows a winged creature with two legs. It shows the creature flying over treetops. People doubt the photo is the Mothman. They think it's a bird with a snake. They think it was taken at a weird angle.

They were driving at around midnight. They were outside of town. The area was called the "TNT area." It was the site of a former World War II gun factory. This factory made things that explode. Woods surround the area. The largest number of Mothman sightings happened near this area.

The couples parked. They say they saw something. They saw a "large flying man" with 10-foot (3 meters) wings. They said it had two large glowing red eyes. They screamed. They drove away.

They say the creature spread its wings. It followed their car. It chased them down the highway. It was fast. It disappeared into the woods.

Teens hung out in the "TNT area."

Mothman liked jumping on the roofs of people's cars.

The couples went to the cops. They told their story. The local news printed their story. The newspaper headline was, "Couple Sees Man-Sized Bird...Creature...Something." After this, many more people reported seeing Mothman.

Marcella Bennett was visiting her friends. She was near the TNT area. She walked to her car. She said she saw giant wings. She saw glowing red eyes. She was scared. She dropped her baby. She fell on top of her baby. Then she ran inside the house. She called the cops. She said Mothman walked to the porch and looked inside the windows.

Chapter Two

FIRE EYES

What does Mothman look like? What happens when people see Mothman?

Point Pleasant, West Virginia, is a small town. It's by the Ohio River. It's the home of the Mothman legend. There were more than 100 Mothman sightings reported between November 1966 and December 1967.

Mothman is a **humanoid**. Humanoids are monsters that look like humans. Mothman is about 7 feet (2 m) tall. It has two legs. It's brown or black. It has glowing red eyes. Some say its eyes are set in its chest. Not much is known about Mothman's face. People are distracted by its eyes. They don't pay attention to its face.

Sketch artists drew Mothman based on many reports.

Mothman liked sleeping in people's backyards.

Mothman has long wings. Its wingspan is over 10 feet (3 m). Its wings are like a **moth**'s. Moths are flying insects. They're similar to butterflies.

Mothman doesn't flap its wings like a bird. It flies like a helicopter. It spreads its wings. It rises. It flies straight up into the air. It flies faster than a bird. On land, it folds its wings. It walks like a penguin. It has a weird shuffle.

Mothman **shrieks**. Shrieks are loud cries. They have a high pitch. They hurt people's ears.

SPOTLIGHT

BIOGRAPHY

Jeff Wamsley owns the Mothman Museum. He opened it in 2005. He helped organize the Mothman Festival. He was born in 1961. He's from Point Pleasant. He remembers growing up during the November 1966 Mothman sightings. He lived next to the Scarberrys. He said, "Even though I was only 5 years old at the time, I remember the stories told by my mother." He started a website about Mothman. The website was popular. Wamsley said, "We knew at that moment the Mothman legend was bigger than ever." He's been in many films, TV shows, and articles about Mothman. He's written some books about Mothman. His goal is to protect his town's story. He said, "I'm still searching, just like everyone else. I know there was something that people were seeing. But I don't know what it is."

Seeing Mothman hurts people. There are **side effects**. Side effects are things that happen to people as a result of something. These side effects never go away. People suffer pain for a long time.

Some people get **physical** pain. Physical refers to people's bodies. Some people get ear pain. Some get eye pain. Some get burns on their skin.

Some people get **mental** pain. Mental refers to the mind. People become extremely fearful. They get mental distress. They lose their minds.

Some people reported seeing pure evil in Mothman's eyes.

Chapter Three

BAD OMEN

How is Mothman a bad omen? What are some disasters connected to Mothman?

Mothman was first reported in the United States in 1966. But Mothman has been around longer than that. In 1926, Mothman appeared in China. Chinese people called it "man-dragon." Mothman was seen by the Xiaon Te Dam. The dam broke. The city flooded. More than 15,000 people died. Some people thought Mothman was a bad **omen**. Omens are signs. Mothman shows up before bad things happened.

This seemed true for Point Pleasant. People said they saw Mothman flying over Silver Bridge. Mothman reports stopped on December 15, 1967. This is when the Silver Bridge fell. This happened during heavy rush hour traffic. Cars fell into the cold river water. Forty-six people died.

Silver Bridge connected West Virginia and Ohio.
The Silver Memorial Bridge replaced it.

Germans call Mothman, the "Freiburg Shrieker."

Experts blamed the poor design of the bridge. They said the bridge wasn't meant to carry that much weight. But some people blamed Mothman. They think Mothman causes bad things to happen. Other people think Mothman is **prophetic**. Prophetic means seeing the future. Mothman seems to know when disasters will happen. It may be trying to warn people.

Mothman was seen at other disasters. On September 10, 1978, Mothman was seen in Freiburg, Germany. There was a group of miners. They said they saw glowing red eyes. Mothman screamed. The miners went home. An hour later, the mine collapsed. This killed many people. But the group that saw Mothman escaped. Mothman saved their lives.

Moths have been known to invade cities. Nan is a county in central China. Swarms of moths attacked the city. They flew around. They gathered under street lamps. The next day, they dropped dead. Billions of dead moth bodies covered the city. A citizen said, "Moths had filled the skies. They flew into my face. They hit the cars. It sounds just like popcorn popping." Shops closed. They turned off their lights. They wanted to get rid of the moths. Some people thought the moths were a bad sign. They thought an earthquake was coming. Scientists denied earthquakes. They said the warm weather caused moth eggs to hatch. Moths go to city lights to mate.

Mothman was called the "Blackbird of Chernobyl."

Mothman was seen in 1985 in Chernobyl in the Soviet Union. On April 26, 1986, there was a big explosion there. There was a **nuclear** disaster. Nuclear is a power source. More than 56 people died. More than 4,000 people got sick.

People saw Mothman flying around the Twin Towers in New York City. They saw it right before September 11, 2001. On that day, terrorists attacked the United States. Planes crashed into the Twin Towers. Many people died.

Mothman was spotted in La Junta, Mexico. Reports started in 2009. That was the year the **swine** flu hit Mexico. Swine means pig. Many people around the world got sick. The most deaths happened in Mexico.

Chapter Four

CURSED LIFE

What are some ideas for how the Mothman legend started? Who is Chief Cornstalk?

Nobody knows where Mothman came from. Some people think Mothman is an alien. People saw **UFOs** at the same time as Mothman. UFOs are unidentified flying objects. They're alien spaceships. People saw dancing red lights. They reported electrical disturbances. This led people to think aliens were involved.

Some people think Mothman is a **mutant**. Mutant means not normal. The TNT area used to be a bird park. Then, it was a gun factory. Lots of chemicals were dumped in the area. This may have created a strange bird-human monster.

Some people think Mothman is an alien or a mutant.

23

Some people think Mothman is part of a Shawnee **curse**. Curses are evil spells. Shawnee tribes lived in the Point Pleasant area. They had stories about Thunderbirds. Thunderbirds swooped down. They carried away men. Mothman is part of these stories.

Chief Cornstalk was a Shawnee leader. He tried to protect his people during the American Revolution. He wanted to get back his lands. Angry soldiers killed him. They killed his son. They killed two other Shawnees. Cornstalk's body was buried in Point Pleasant. People say he took **revenge** by sending Mothman. Revenge means getting even.

Mothman may be a modern-day Thunderbird.

INVESTIGATION TIPS

- Talk to someone who's seen Mothman.

- Do an Internet search. Read many witness reports. Pay attention to details that are the same.

- Go to the Mothman Museum. Look at all the exhibits. Exhibits are things shown in museums. Study each item. Read about it. Take notes.

- Go to the Mothman Festival. Learn from the speakers. Meet other people who are interested in Mothman.

- Don't trust photos. Remember, photos can be changed.

- Watch documentaries about Mothman. Documentaries are films about real events and real people. They're not fiction. They're true. But they have a bias. Bias is a person's opinion or way of seeing things.

Chapter Five

JUST BORING BIRDS

How do scientists explain Mothman? How do pranksters connect to Mothman?

Scientists don't believe in Mothman. They think people are really seeing birds.

Some people think Mothman is an **albino** owl. Albino means not having color. Albino owls have red eyes. Car headlights or flashlights hit the owl's eyes. Their red eyes look like they're glowing.

Dr. Robert L. Smith is a wildlife **biologist**. Biologists study animals. Smith thinks Mothman is a sandhill crane. The crane is tall. Its wingspan is 7 feet (2 m). It has red around its eyes. Smith thinks people didn't recognize the bird. So they made up Mothman stories.

Sandhill cranes can make loud screeching sounds.

EXPLAINED BY SCIENCE

Light rays travel through the eye. They hit the retina. They bounce back from the retina. Retina is sensitive tissue. It detects light. It's at the back of the eye. It takes in images. It sends signals to the brain. It tells the brain what to see. Eyes adjust to different lights. Some eyes are red in pictures. This is called the "red-eye effect." It happens when camera flashes are used at night. It happens in dim lighting. Cameras flash. Eyes don't have time to reduce the light coming in. A large burst of light hits the retina. It hits the red blood vessels. It bounces back. It's caught on film. It makes eyes look red.

George Johnson worked in Point Pleasant. He was the sheriff during the sightings. He thought Mothman was a large heron.

Some blame **pranksters**. Pranksters play jokes on people. They like to trick people. A local man dressed in a costume. He hung around the TNT area. He pretended to be Mothman. He liked scaring people.

Other pranksters got balloons. They filled them up with special gas. They tied red flashlights to them. The balloons floated slowly. They looked like glowing red eyes.

Real or not? It doesn't matter. Mothman lives in people's imaginations.

Some people think Mothman was a plane.

DID YOU KNOW?

Point Pleasant hosted the first Mothman Festival in 2002. It happens every year. It's on the third weekend of September. It has guest speakers. It has a Mothman pancake-eating contest. It has hayride tours.

Bob Roach created a 12-foot-tall (3.6 m) statue of Mothman. He made it out of steel. He finished it in 2003. The statue was placed next to the Mothman Museum.

Chinese people think moths are symbols of death. They think moths are the souls of people who died. It's bad luck to kill or mess with moths.

Some people who saw Mothman reported being visited by "men in black." They say these men wore all black and threatened them. The men told them not to say a word about Mothman.

On November 13, 1966, Merle Partridge heard a loud noise. He lived 90 miles (145 km) from Point Pleasant. His TV made a whining sound. His dog barked wildly. He went outside. He saw two glowing red eyes. His dog went after it. He never saw his dog again.

Awohali is a Cherokee man. He and his son were driving. He was in Wisconsin. He claims Mothman attacked them. This happened in 2006.

Mothman was seen at another bridge collapse. It was in 2007. This took place in Minneapolis, Minnesota. The bridge fell during rush hour. Thirteen people died, and 145 got hurt.

CONSIDER THIS!

Take a Position: Do you think Mothman is good or evil? Does he warn people of danger? Or does he cause danger? Argue your point with reasons and evidence.

Say What? Read the 45th Parallel Press books about vampires and Bigfoot. Compare Mothman to these monsters. Explain how they are similar. Explain how they are different.

Think About It! Learn about humanoids. Create your own humanoid. Draw a picture of it. Give it a name. Describe its strengths and weaknesses. Describe its origination story. Origination means how it was born or formed. Be creative.

LEARN MORE

- Gerhard, Ken. *Encounters with Flying Humanoids: Mothman, Manbirds, Gargoyles & Other Winged Beasts.* Woodbury, MN: Llewellyn Press, 2013.

- Pearce, Q. L. *Mothman.* Detroit: KidHaven, 2010.

- Strange, Jason, and Phil Parks (illus.). *The Mothman's Shadow.* Mankato, MN: Stone Arch Books, 2011.

GLOSSARY

albino (al-BYE-noh) not having any color

biologist (bye-AH-luh-jist) scientist who studies animals

curse (KURS) evil spell

grave (GRAVE) specific site where a dead body is buried

humanoid (HYOO-muh-noyd) monster that has a human shape

mental (MEN-tuhl) of the mind

moth (MAWTH) flying insect that is like a butterfly

mutant (MYOO-tuhnt) not normal

nuclear (NOO-klee-ur) a power source

omen (OH-men) sign, usually a bad sign

physical (FIZ-ih-kuhl) of the body

pranksters (PRANGK-sturz) people who like playing jokes or pranks

prophetic (pruh-FEH-tik) being able to see or predict the future

revenge (rih-VENJ) to get even

shrieks (SHREEKS) high-pitched screaming sounds

side effects (SIDE ih-FEKTS) results of doing or eating something, aftermath

swine (SWINE) pig

UFOs (YOO EF OHZ) unidentified flying objects, alien spaceships

INDEX

ABOUT THE AUTHOR

Dr. Virginia Loh-Hagan is an author, university professor, former classroom teacher, and curriculum designer. She was born and raised in Virginia. She's never been to West Virginia. She lives in San Diego with her very tall husband and very naughty dogs. To learn more about her, visit www.virginialoh.com.